Growing Readers

Purchased with Smart Start Funds

DOCTORS

PEOPLE WHO CARE FOR OUR HEALTH

Robert James

The Rourke Book Co., Inc.
Vero Beach, Florida 32964

PHOTO CREDITS
Cover, pages. 8, 12, 13,17, 21, © Kyle Carter; title page, pages 4,
7, 10, 15 courtesy Mercy Center, Aurora, IL; page 18 courtesy
Wheaton Eye Clinic, Wheaton, IL

Library of Congress Cataloging-in-Publication Data

James, Robert, 1942-
    Doctors / by Robert James.
        p. cm. — (People who care for our health)
    Includes index.
    Summary: Describes what doctors do, where they work, and
how they train and prepare for their jobs.
    ISBN 1-55916-166-3
    1. Medicine—Vocational guidance—Juvenile literature.
[1. Medicine—Vocational guidance. 2. Occupations.
3. Vocational guidance]
I. Title II. Series: James, Robert, 1942- People who care for our
health
R690.J34 1995
610.69—dc20   95–18943
                                                                   CIP
                                                                    AC

Printed in the USA

TABLE OF CONTENTS

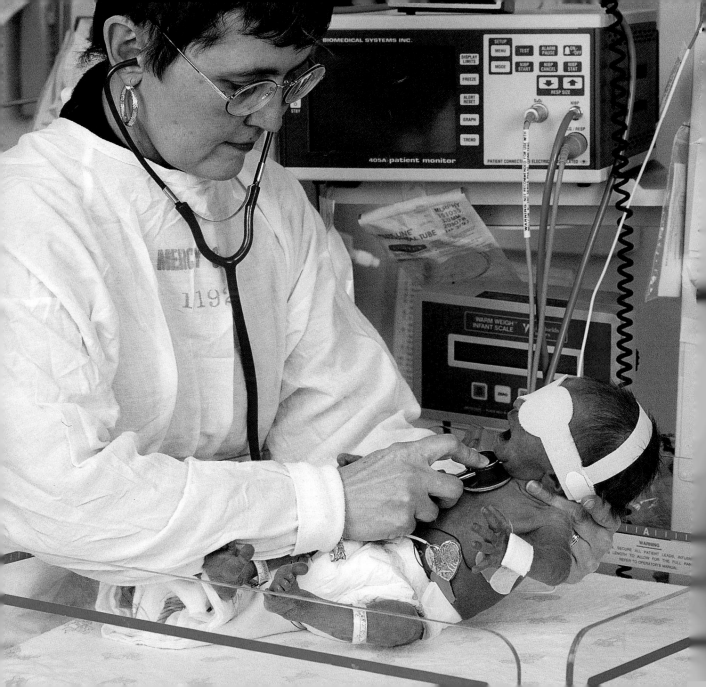

DOCTORS

No one is healthy all the time. When problems with our health arise, we often seek a doctor's expert help.

Doctors are the highly skilled medical people who find out what is wrong with us and treat the problem. Doctors also help people prevent disease and injury.

Nearly 400,000 medical doctors work in the United States and Canada.

Doctors provide expert medical care and counsel to millions of patients of all ages

THE STUDY OF MEDICINE

Medical doctors study and **practice** (PRAHK tiss), or work with, **medicine** (MEH dih sin). "Medicine" is a name for the drugs people take to fight disease or pain. "Medicine" also refers to the study and skill of healing people.

Doctors are experts in ways to cure. The curing skills of doctors help save their patients' lives. Doctors' skills can also help suffering people to feel better.

A doctor who is a heart specialist helps a heart attack victim recover

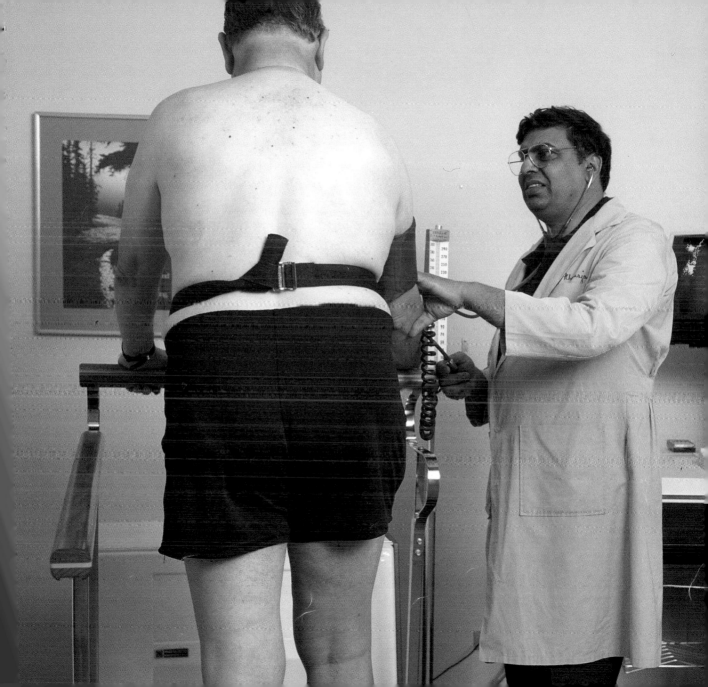

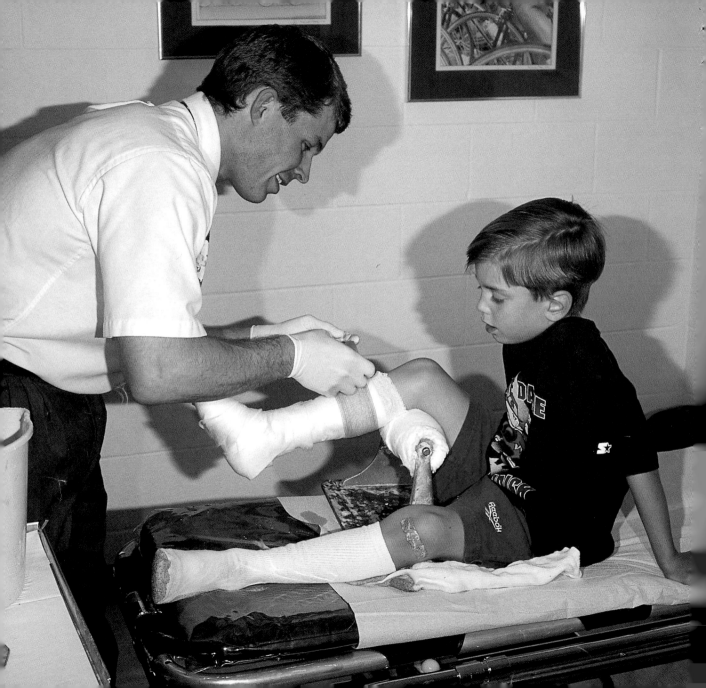

WHAT DOCTORS DO

Medical doctors (MD's) perform many different tasks. Most medical doctors work directly with their patients, people with a concern about their health.

Other medical doctors work "behind the scenes." They may be in a laboratory, where they try to find cures for disease. They may be medical teachers and work with students who wish to be doctors.

Doctors also manage some hospitals and medical schools.

Most doctors deal directly with patients and their problems, like a broken ankle

WHAT'S WRONG?

Most people take serious health problems to a doctor. The doctor studies the patient to learn what is wrong. What a doctor learns is called a **diagnosis** (di ag NO sis)—a decision about the cause of the problem.

Some illnesses are mysteries. A doctor, though, is a detective. The doctor gathers clues about the illness by asking questions and performing tests.

A technician studies the three-dimensional pictures of a person's insides during an MRI test ordered by the doctor

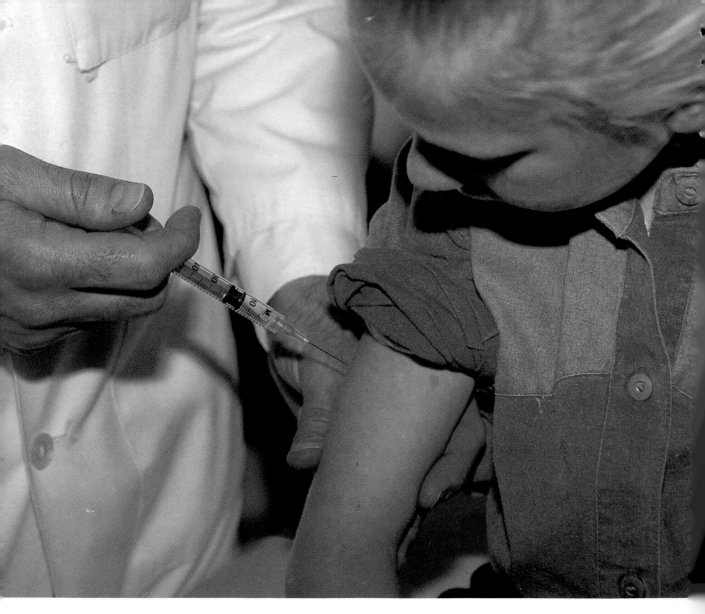

Drug injections ordered by the doctor will protect this girl from many childhood diseases

*Doctors continue learning about their art long after they have
earned their college degrees*

TREATMENT

Doctors are trained to solve health mysteries. With time and testing, they can usually make a diagnosis. Then a doctor can begin another important part of the job—treatment.

A doctor has many ways to treat patients who are ill. The doctor may order the use of drugs or special machines to treat someone. In some cases, the doctor may perform **surgery** (SUR jer ee) or send the patient to another health care **specialist** (SPESH ul ihst).

14

A radiologist technician (left) assists a heart specialist performing surgery in a hospital operating room

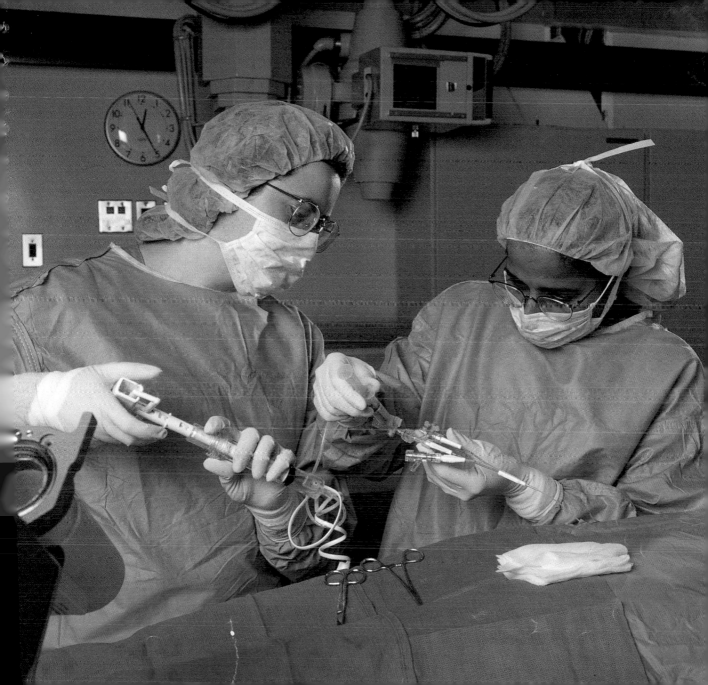

KINDS OF DOCTORS

Surgery is another word for operation. During surgery, a doctor cuts into some part of the body. A surgeon is a doctor who performs surgery.

Many kinds of surgeons and non-surgeons are specialists. They study and treat health problems of a special type or body part, such as the brain or eyes.

About one American doctor in five is a general **practitioner** (PRAHK tish un er), or family doctor. These doctors take patients of all ages and with all types of problems.

A family doctor checks for signs of an infection in a young patient's ears

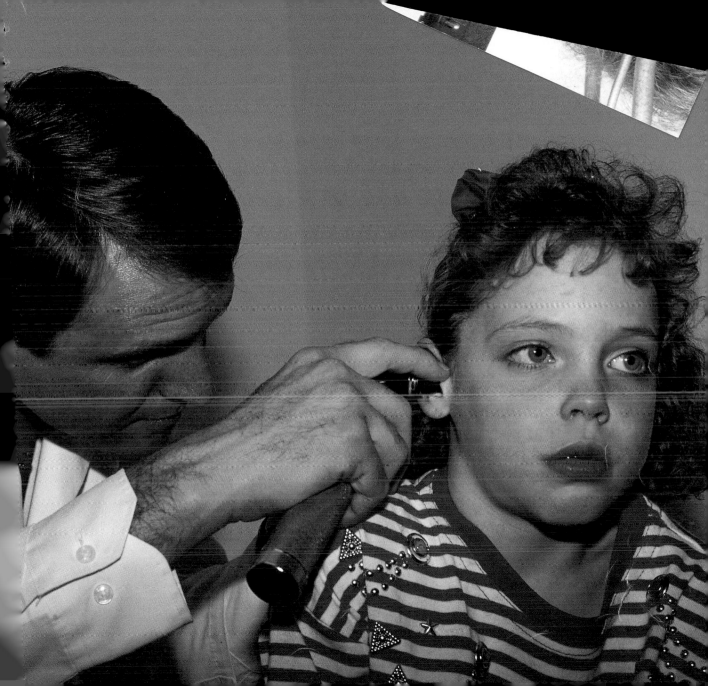

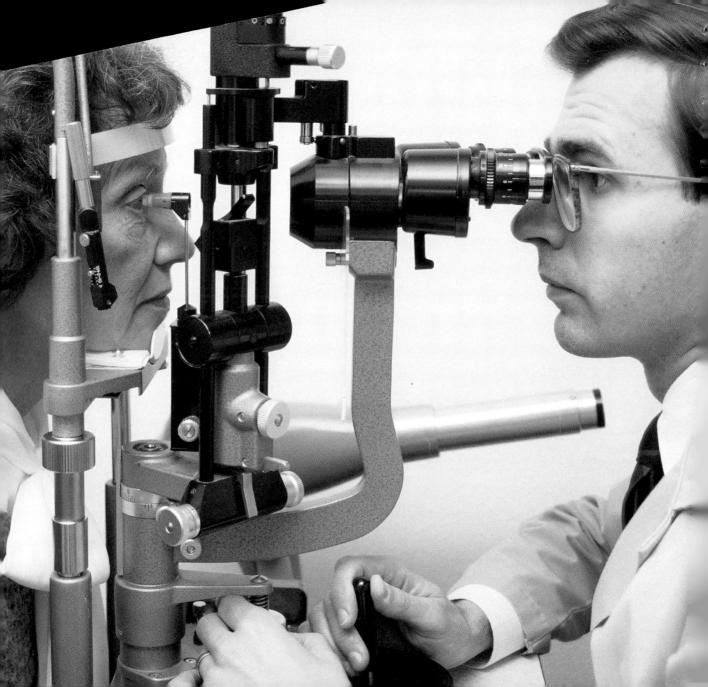

WHERE DOCTORS WORK

Doctors work in private offices, hospitals, or clinics. Most hospital doctors also have their own practices and spend time in their offices.

A doctor may work in partnership with another doctor or a group of doctors. A large group of doctors may work in a clinic.

Each clinic usually has several specialists. Clinics usually have their own laboratories and a variety of medical machines.

Seeing eye to eye with his patient, an eye specialist doctor tests for eye disease in an eye care clinic

19

A DOCTOR'S HELPERS

Doctors work closely with other health care **professionals** (pro FESH un ulz). Professionals are highly trained people.

Doctors and several other professionals make up health care teams. Each member of a team has a special task.

Medical technicians, for example, help operate medical machines. Nurses help surgeons at work and with the day-to-day care of patients. **Pharmacists** (FARM uh sists) prepare the drugs a doctor orders.

Doctors also work with many other health care professionals.

A doctor (right) discusses with a nurse the medical treatment of a patient

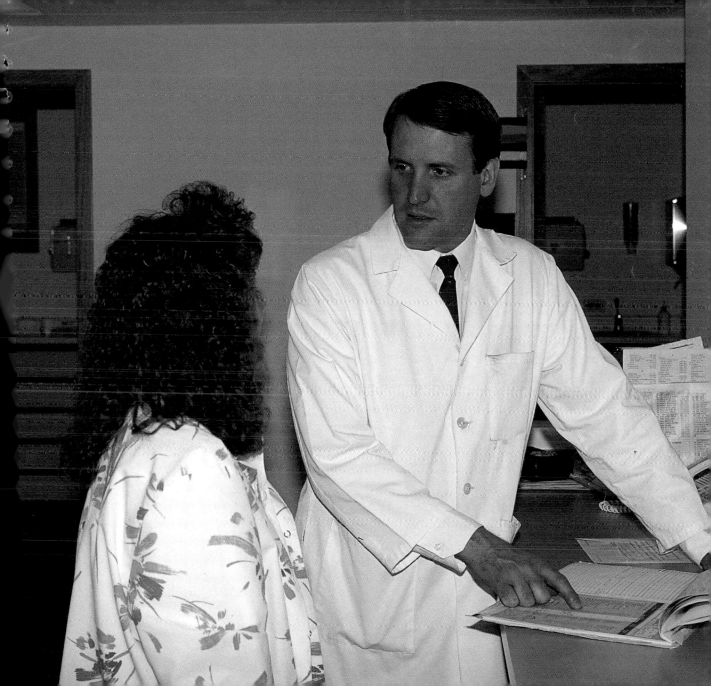

BECOMING A DOCTOR

Becoming a doctor is difficult and costly. A doctor has to spend eight years in college. Then a doctor works for two years in on-the-job training at a hospital.

A doctor's life, however, can be rewarding. Doctors save lives and make people feel better. They are masters of healing.

In addition, doctors are usually well paid and highly respected.

Glossary

diagnosis (di ag NO sis) — the act and process by which a doctor figures out an illness; the doctor's decision about the nature of an illness

medicine (MEH dih sin) — the study of healing and the skill involved in the act of healing; a medical drug

pharmacist (FARM uh sist) — one who studies and prepares drugs

practice (PRAHK tiss) — to work as a medical doctor or other professional; the professional's private business

practitioner (PRAHK tish un er) — one who practices or works at a profession, such as medicine

professional (pro FESH un ul) — one who is highly trained, highly skilled, and paid for his or her work

specialist (SPESH ul ihst) — a doctor whose work deals with a fairly small, special area of the body

surgery (SUR jer ee) — a medical operation; a medical act that cuts into some part of the body

INDEX